How to Stop Losing Money

Ricardo Moreno

Ricardo Moreno

Index

Mindset Before Strategy

Trading may seem like an exciting game. You watch the charts go up and down, you hear stories of people who made fortunes, and you imagine yourself achieving that financial freedom you long for. But let me tell you something: if your main focus is to make money quickly, you are starting on the wrong path. Before learning strategies, patterns, or indicators, you need to work on the most important thing: your mindset. Because without the right mindset, no strategy will be enough to avoid losses.

When you start trading, your first impulse is usually to look for ways to make more. That's natural. But have you ever stopped to think about how not to lose? This is the true art of trading: protecting what you have before trying to multiply it. A defensive mindset in trading isn't sexy, it's not exciting, but it's the only thing that can keep you in the game. And the truth is, this game isn't about winning a single spectacular trade; it's about surviving the inevitable losses and moving forward.

I want you to think about this: the market doesn't owe you anything. It doesn't care how much you need to make this month to pay your bills or achieve your dreams. It's a neutral system, full of opportunities and dangers. Most traders lose because they approach the market with the wrong expectations, believing they can control it or that they must win every time they trade. This belief is a perfect recipe for disaster.

One of the biggest enemies of your trading progress is yourself. It's that inner voice that tells you, "This time it will be different," while you ignore all the warning signs. It's the impatience that leads you to enter poorly planned trades just because you feel like you're missing out. It's the frustration after a loss that pushes you to make impulsive decisions to "win back" what you lost. And worst of all: it's the arrogance after a winning streak that makes you forget about the risks. If you don't control these emotions, the market will do it for you, and believe me, it won't be kind.

So how do you build a defensive mindset? It all starts with accepting a reality that many find hard to swallow: losses are part of trading. No matter how good you are, you're going to have losses. The problem isn't losing; the problem is how you react to those losses. A trader with the right mindset sees them as the cost of doing business, as an opportunity to learn. A trader with the wrong mindset sees them as a personal affront, as a character flaw. This difference in perspective can determine whether you survive or fall by the wayside.

Patience is another key element. In trading, doing nothing is just as important as taking action. Inexperienced traders feel that they always have to be trading, that every market movement is an opportunity. But the reality is that it isn't. The best traders know how to wait. They observe, analyze, and only act when everything is aligned in their favor. Trading out of boredom, anxiety, or personal pressure is one of the quickest ways to lose money.

You also need to develop the skill of emotionally detaching yourself from each trade. This sounds easy in theory, but it's challenging in practice. Every time you place a trade, there's a part of you that expects to win. It's natural, but dangerous. When you're emotionally attached to a trade, it's harder to close a losing position or stay calm if things don't go your way. This is where discipline comes in. You have to learn to follow your rules, even when your mind tells you "this time you can break them."

I want you to think of trading as if you were the captain of a ship sailing on an unpredictable ocean. You can't control the weather or the waves, but you can control how you prepare your ship and how you respond to storms. Your capital is that ship. If you take unnecessary risks, don't check your maps, or don't correct course in time, the ship will sink. Your primary responsibility isn't to get to the destination faster; it's to make sure the ship stays afloat.

The real secret to trading isn't finding the perfect strategy. It's learning how to manage yourself. It's knowing when to trade and when to sit out. It's recognizing that the market isn't your enemy, but it's not your friend either. It's a neutral ground that can reward or punish you depending on how you behave. And here's the key point: if you focus on protecting your capital, rather than chasing quick profits, you'll be giving yourself the opportunity to keep learning and improving.

Trading is not a sprint; it is an endurance test. It is not about winning today or tomorrow, but about continuing to trade consistently for years. Strategy can wait. First you need to build a mindset that will allow you to survive the journey. And remember: the goal is not to win every time. The goal is to not lose in a way that takes you out of the game. Once you internalize this, you will be ready to learn the strategies and tools that really make a difference.

The Golden Rules of Risk Control

In the trading world, risk management is like a seatbelt in a car. You can be an excellent driver, know every curve on the road, and have the fastest car, but if you don't wear your seatbelt, the first accident could be your last. That's how important it is to protect your capital. It doesn't matter how good your strategy is or how safe a trade seems; if you don't manage risk properly, you're playing with fire. And in trading, fire burns fast.

The most common mistake among traders, especially beginners, is to think about how much they can win instead of focusing on how much they can lose. This approach is a dangerous trap. Before entering any trade, you need to be clear about how much you are willing to risk and what you will do if things don't go your way. This is not optional; it is the foundation of any successful trade. If you don't know how much you can lose before you open a position, you are walking blindly into a minefield.

The first rule of thumb is to never risk more than you are willing to lose. It seems obvious, but many traders forget it as soon as they see an opportunity that is "sure to work out." Here's the problem: in trading, there are no guarantees. Even seemingly perfect trades can go wrong. That's why you should set a clear loss limit for every trade. A commonly accepted rule is to risk no more than 1% of your total capital on a single trade. This means that if you have a $10,000 account, your maximum loss on a trade should be $100. This limit may seem small, but it is precisely what will keep you in the game in the long run.

Another fundamental rule is to define your daily and weekly loss limits. Let's say you have a bad day and hit your daily loss limit. The smartest thing you can do is stop. Yes, I know it hurts to admit that the day didn't go the way you wanted, but forcing more trades to try to recover what you lost almost always ends in more losses. The same applies on a weekly basis. If you have a losing streak, take a step back, evaluate what's going on, and get back into the market with a clear mind. Remember, trading is a marathon, not a sprint.

Let's talk about stop losses, those little heroes that many traders ignore until it's too late. A stop loss is an order that automatically closes your position when the price hits a predetermined loss level. Simply put, it's your escape plan if things go south. But here's the key: there's no point in setting a stop loss if you don't respect it. One of the worst mistakes you can make is moving your stop loss further out to "give your trade room." This almost always ends in a bigger loss. Be disciplined. If the price hits your stop loss, accept the loss and move on.

In addition to your stop loss, it's important to consider your position size. This is where many traders get into trouble. They see a trade that looks promising and bet a disproportionate amount of their account. This is extremely dangerous. Your position size should be aligned with the risk you're willing to take. For example, if you're willing to risk $100 on a trade and your stop loss is 10 points away from your entry price, then your position size should be 10 contracts or shares (depending on the market). It's simple math, but many ignore it because they're thinking about how much they could make instead of how much they could lose.

Another crucial aspect of risk control is avoiding excessive use of leverage. Leverage can be a double-edged sword. Yes, it can magnify your profits, but it also amplifies your losses. And if you don't manage it carefully, you can lose more than you have in your account. Before using leverage, make sure you fully understand how it works and adjust your positions so that the risk remains manageable. Never use leverage just because it allows you to trade with more money than you have; use it as a strategic tool, not a shortcut to making more.

Risk control also means knowing when not to trade. Sometimes the best way to protect your capital is to simply stay out of the market. If you are emotionally affected, tired, or don't understand what is going on in the market, don't trade. Trading in these conditions is like playing poker without looking at your cards. You have no idea what you are doing, and the odds are stacked against you.

Finally, remember that risk management is not something you do once and then forget about. It is a habit you must cultivate on every trade, every day. It requires discipline and sometimes willpower to close a losing position or accept that today is not your day. But that same discipline is what will allow you to stay in the game in the long run and eventually achieve success.

Risk control is not about eliminating all losses; that is impossible. It is about making sure that no loss is big enough to take you out of the market. In trading, protecting your capital should always be your number one priority. By following these golden rules, you will be building a solid foundation that will allow you to face the ups and downs of the market with confidence and control.

How to Choose a Safe Position Size

Choosing the right position size is one of the most important decisions you'll make as a trader. In fact, this step is what separates responsible traders from those who end up destroying their account in a matter of days. Many times, when traders lose money, it's not because their strategy is terrible, but because they risked too much on a single trade. This is where the art of safe position sizing comes in, a skill that not only protects your capital, but also gives you the peace of mind to make rational decisions.

The first thing you need to understand is that your position size should be directly related to the risk you are willing to take on each trade. A commonly used rule is the 1% rule. This means that on each trade, you should not risk more than 1% of your total capital. For example, if you have a $10,000 account, your maximum loss per trade should be $100. This limit may seem conservative, but it ensures that one losing streak does not wipe out your account.

Now, how does this translate into your position size? This is where you need some basic math. Let's say you're trading an asset and you decide that your stop loss will be 10 points away from your entry price. This means that if the market moves 10 points against you, you will exit the trade. If your maximum risk is $100, then your position size should be such that each point of movement costs you $10. In this case, you would trade 10 contracts, shares, or units, depending on the market you're in.

Now let's talk about why it's so important to stick to this calculation. Imagine that you decide to ignore this rule and trade with twice the recommended size because you feel like "this trade will be a winner." If things go wrong, instead of losing $100, you'll now be losing $200. It may not seem like a big deal, but if you repeat this mistake over and over again, your account will quickly dwindle. Trading is not a game of emotions; it's a game of probabilities. And trading with proper position sizing is what ensures that the odds are in your favor in the long run.

The next important point is leverage. Leverage allows you to trade with more money than you actually have in your account, which can be tempting, but also extremely dangerous. If you don't match your position size to the risk you're willing to take, leverage can amplify your losses in devastating ways. For example, if you use 10:1 leverage and lose 1% of the asset's value, you've actually lost 10% of your account. Before using leverage, make sure you understand its risks and carefully calculate your position size.

Another factor to consider is market volatility. Not all assets move the same way. Some have larger, sharper moves, while others are more stable. If you are trading a highly volatile asset, your stop loss will likely be further away to allow room for natural price movements. This means your position size will need to be smaller to keep risk under control. On the other hand, if you are trading a less volatile asset, you can afford a larger position size without increasing your risk.

It is also crucial to review your position size if your account grows or shrinks. If you start with a $10,000 account and apply the 1% rule, your trades will be limited to a risk of $100. But if your account drops to $8,000, you should now be risking $80 per trade. This may seem frustrating, but it is a necessary measure to protect your capital.

Similarly, if your account grows to $15,000, you can increase the risk per trade to $150, always respecting the same percentage.

One of the keys to choosing a safe position size is consistency. You can't change your rules every time you feel like "this trade will be different." The market doesn't work like that, and the more you change your rules, the more likely you are to make mistakes. Define a clear method for calculating your position size and stick to it on every trade. Discipline is what turns average traders into successful traders.

Finally, remember that position sizing not only protects your account, it also protects your mindset. When you trade with proper size, you can accept losses as part of the process without feeling like your world is falling apart. This is critical, because uncontrolled emotions are one of a trader's biggest enemies. If you find yourself trading with a position size that makes you feel overly anxious or keeps you up at night, it's a sign that you're risking too much.

Choosing a safe position size may seem like a boring topic compared to trading strategies and charts, but it is one of the fundamental pillars of success. Without proper management of your position sizes, even the best strategy will fail. Take the time to learn and apply this skill. In the long run, your account, your confidence, and your trading career will thank you for it.

Common Mistakes That Destroy Capital

Trading has a way of humiliating those who underestimate it. What starts out as an activity filled with excitement and expectations of huge profits can quickly turn into a nightmare if you're not careful. And the main reason is not the market, but the mistakes we traders make. These mistakes are not only common, but devastating. They can destroy your capital before you even realize what you're doing wrong. If you want to survive in the trading world, you must first learn to recognize and avoid these mistakes.

One of the most common and dangerous mistakes is trading without a plan. Entering the market without a clear strategy is like jumping into a boat without oars in the middle of a storm. Every trade you make should be part of a predefined plan, including your entry and exit rules, position sizing, and risk management. But many traders, especially beginners, enter the market because they feel like they "have to do something" or because "this opportunity looks good." Trading this way is like playing the lottery. You might get lucky once or twice, but in the long run, you will lose more than you win.

Another common mistake is overtrading. This happens when you enter too many trades, often without valid reasons. Sometimes it's because you're bored, sometimes it's because you're trying to recoup a recent loss, and sometimes it's simply because you think the more you trade, the more money you'll make. But trading doesn't work like that. More trades don't mean more profits, and every time you enter the market, you're taking a risk. Overtrading not only drains your account, but it also wears you down emotionally, leading you to make even more mistakes.

Lack of discipline is another deadly enemy of the trader. This manifests itself in many ways: ignoring your stop loss, moving it further out to avoid a loss, not following your own rules, or staying in a trade longer than necessary because "the market has to turn." Every time you break a rule, you're sending a message to yourself that emotions are in charge, not your plan. And in trading, acting impulsively is a recipe for disaster. Discipline is not optional; it's the foundation of every successful trader.

Excessive leverage is another mistake that destroys accounts quickly. Leverage may seem appealing because it allows you to control more money than you actually have, but it also amplifies losses. Many new traders are tempted by the possibility of making large amounts in a short time and forget that leverage is unforgiving. One bad trade with high leverage can wipe out weeks, even months of profits, in a matter of minutes. If you don't understand how to use leverage responsibly, you're better off not using it at all.

Then there is the problem of not accepting losses. No trader, no matter how good, wins on every trade. However, some traders refuse to accept that they have made a mistake and let losses mount, hoping that the market will "bounce back." This is extremely dangerous. Every trade you make should have a clear limit on how much you are willing to lose. If the price hits that point, you should get out, no excuses. Holding on to a losing trade not only costs you money, but it also affects your confidence and ability to make rational decisions in the future.

Another classic mistake is trading based on emotions like fear and greed. For example, after a loss, it's common to feel the need to "make up" your losses quickly. This can lead you to enter into impulsive trades, without properly analyzing the market. On the other hand, after a winning streak, it's easy to feel invincible and start taking unnecessary risks, such as increasing your position size or ignoring your rules. In both cases, emotions cloud your judgment and push you to make unwise decisions.

Lack of preparation is another serious problem. Many traders enter the market without really understanding what they are doing. They don't study the assets they trade, they don't take the time to analyze the market, and they don't test their strategies before using them with real money. Trading is not a game; it's a business. And like any business, it requires preparation, study, and practice. If you are not willing to invest time in learning, the market will make you pay for it with losses.

There is also the mistake of ignoring capital management. Many traders think only about potential profits and forget to protect their money. They don't use stop losses, risk too much on a single trade, or fail to diversify their risks. But trading isn't just about how much you can make, it's about how much you can keep. Protecting your capital is rule number one, because without capital, you can't trade.

Finally, one of the most insidious mistakes is not keeping a record of your trades. If you don't keep a trading journal where you write down every trade, including why you made it, how it went, and what you learned, you're missing out on one of the most valuable tools for improvement. A journal helps you identify patterns in your behavior, both positive and negative, and allows you to correct mistakes before they become destructive habits.

Trading is a mental game as much as a technical one. Common mistakes that destroy money don't always have to do with failed strategies, but rather with impulsive decisions, lack of discipline, and the wrong mindset. Learning to recognize these mistakes, and most importantly, correct them, is what will make the difference between being a trader who survives and thrives, or one who falls by the wayside. Remember, you can't control the market, but you can control how you behave in it.

And that is what will ultimately determine your success.

The Power of Stop Loss

In the world of trading, few tools are as important and yet as underrated as the stop loss. For many beginners, the concept of voluntarily accepting a loss seems foreign or even unnecessary. Why would I close a losing trade when the market could turn in my favor at any moment? This mindset is the beginning of a downward spiral. Not using a stop loss is like driving without brakes on a winding road. You may get to your destination a few times, but sooner or later you will have an accident.

A stop loss is not just a button on your trading platform; it is your lifeline in the market. It is an automatic order that is triggered when the price reaches a predefined level, closing your position to limit losses. But its true power is not only in protecting your capital, but also in protecting your mindset. Without a stop loss, every trade becomes a constant emotional tug-of-war, where doubt, fear and hope take over. With a stop loss, you free your mind from that burden.

One of the biggest mistakes traders make is thinking they can "monitor" their trades instead of using a stop loss. They tell themselves they will be vigilant and close the trade manually if things go wrong. But the reality is that when price is moving rapidly against you, it's easy to freeze up or fall into the magical thinking that "everything will get better." Before you know it, the loss you could have controlled has spiraled out of control. A stop loss eliminates this uncertainty by acting emotionlessly, just when you need it most.

Setting a stop loss doesn't mean you accept that you're losing, it means you accept that you have no control over the market. No trader, no matter how experienced, can accurately predict every market move. There will be times when the market will go against you, no matter how good your strategy is or how much research you've done. A stop loss isn't an admission of defeat, but rather a tool to protect you from the unexpected.

One of the keys to using stop losses effectively is to place them in a strategic location. You shouldn't set a stop loss based solely on a random number, such as losing $50 or $100. Instead, it should be based on market logic, such as key support or resistance levels, technical patterns, or recent volatility. This ensures that the stop loss is far enough away to give the price room to move naturally, but not so far away that you risk too much capital.

Another important aspect is not moving your stop loss once you have set it. This is a common mistake that can be disastrous. Imagine you decide to move your stop loss further because you think the market will "surely" turn in your favor. What you are actually doing is increasing your risk without any guarantee that things will improve. If the price hits your original stop loss, it means your analysis was wrong. Accept the loss and move on. Moving your stop loss is not a solution; it is an excuse to avoid facing reality.

Stop losses also help you maintain discipline during times of high volatility. Markets can be chaotic, especially during news events or periods of economic uncertainty. At these times, prices can move quickly, making even the most experienced traders feel nervous. Having a stop loss in place means you don't need to make impulsive decisions in the heat of the moment. Your plan is already in place, and your risk is controlled.

Additionally, using a stop loss allows you to think of trading as a game of probability. You don't need to win on every trade to be profitable. In fact, many successful traders have a success rate of only 50% or less. What makes them profitable isn't the number of winning trades, but how they handle losses. A stop loss ensures that no loss is large enough to erase the profits from several successful trades.

The power of stop losses also extends to your confidence as a trader. When you know you have a mechanism in place to limit your losses, you can trade with less fear. This doesn't mean you become careless, but it does mean you can make decisions without the constant worry that a single trade will ruin your account. This level of confidence is essential to trading consistently and objectively.

It's important to mention that not using a stop loss also affects your account in the long run. A single big loss can take you weeks or months of profits to recover, and that's if you're lucky enough not to completely wipe out your account. On the other hand, using a stop loss allows you to keep your capital relatively stable, even during difficult periods. This means that you can stay in the game long enough to learn, improve, and take advantage of future opportunities.

Some traders complain that the market often seems to “hunt” their stop losses before moving in the expected direction. While this can be frustrating, it is often a sign that the stop loss was placed at a level that was too obvious or too close. This can be fixed by adjusting your stop loss levels more carefully and considering factors such as market volatility. But even if your stop loss is occasionally triggered, remember that it is serving its purpose: limiting your losses.

Trading is not about avoiding all losses – that is impossible. It is about controlling how much you lose when things don’t go your way. That is the essence of the stop loss. It is not a magic tool that guarantees success, but it is a shield that protects you from yourself and the unpredictable nature of the market. If you learn to use it effectively, you will not only protect your capital, but you will also improve your mindset and discipline as a trader.

At its core, the power of stop losses lies in the freedom they give you. They free you from the anxiety of constantly monitoring the market, from the destructive emotions that arise when a trade goes wrong, and from the possibility that a single wrong decision can destroy your account. Don't underestimate this tool. It's one of the few things in trading that is truly within your control. And in a market where control is at a premium, that's invaluable.

The Importance of Patience in Entry

Patience is one of the most underrated qualities in trading, especially when it comes to market entries. In a world where everything seems to spin at breakneck speeds and where markets are constantly on the move, waiting for the right moment to enter can seem like a waste of time. But here's the truth: patience in entry is not just a virtue, it's a strategic tool that separates consistent traders from those who are simply gambling.

Imagine you are hunting in a forest. You don't shoot at anything that moves, do you? You first observe, study the environment, analyze the behavior of your prey and wait for the perfect moment to act. In trading, the situation is similar. If you enter the market at any time, without waiting for a clear signal or confirmation of your analysis, you will most likely end up on the wrong side of the trade.

Many traders, especially beginners, feel pressured to be constantly in the market. They think that every minute they are not trading is a lost opportunity. This mindset leads them to enter impulsive trades, without solid justification or proper analysis. But the reality is that the market will always be there. There will always be another opportunity. The problem is not missing a potential trade, but entering at the wrong time and ending up losing money.

Patience in entry starts with having a clear plan. Before you even look at the charts, you need to know exactly what you're looking for. Maybe it's a technical pattern, a breakout of a key level, or a confirmation on an indicator. Whatever it is, you need to have a clear picture in your mind of what your ideal trade should look like. And then, you need to wait until that picture materializes in the market. This can be frustrating, especially when you see the price moving and feel like you're missing out on something. But entering too early, just out of impatience, usually results in losses.

A common mistake among impatient traders is chasing the price. This happens when you see the market moving quickly in one direction and instead of waiting for a pullback or confirmation, you decide to enter impulsively out of fear of missing out on the opportunity. The problem is that the market doesn't move in a straight line. Even in a strong trend, there will be pullbacks and consolidations. If you enter at the wrong time, just before a pullback, you'll end up stuck in a losing trade, even if the overall move is going in the direction you expected.

Another key aspect of patience is waiting for the market to confirm your analysis. Sometimes, you have a clear idea of what might happen, but the market hasn't yet given any signs that it's going in that direction. For example, you might identify an important resistance level and anticipate that the price will reverse when it hits it. But if you enter before the price shows signs of reversal, you're taking unnecessary risks. Maybe the price will break through the resistance and continue to rise, and you'll be stuck in a losing trade.

Patience in entry is also closely tied to emotional control. It's easy to feel anxious when you're staring at the screen, watching prices constantly move. It may seem like everyone else is making money while you wait. But this is where you need to remember that trading is not a race. It's not about who makes the most trades, but who makes the smartest decisions. Every time you feel the temptation to rush, pause and ask yourself if you're acting on your plan or on your emotions.

A practical way to cultivate patience is to set clear rules for your entries. For example, if you are trading a breakout, you can decide that you will only enter after the price closes above a key level and confirms the move in the next time frame. These rules help you avoid impulsiveness and wait for ideal conditions. Yes, you may lose some trades because the market moves without giving you the confirmation you were hoping for. But you will also avoid many bad trades that would have resulted in losses.

Also, it's important to remember that patience doesn't mean inactivity. While you're waiting for the perfect entry, you can use that time to analyze the market, adjust your plan, and mentally prepare. Waiting isn't wasted time; it's an investment in making better-informed decisions.

You should also understand that being patient does not guarantee that all of your trades will be winners. There will be times when you wait patiently for a perfect setup, enter the market, and still lose. This is part of trading. Patience does not eliminate risk, but it does reduce it by ensuring that you only take trades that make sense from the perspective of your strategy.

Finally, remember that trading is not about trading all the time, but about trading well. A patient trader may make fewer trades, but his success rate will be higher because each entry will be carefully selected. Patience is a form of discipline, and discipline is what separates profitable traders from losing traders in the long run.

At its core, patience in entry isn't just a technical skill, it's a mindset. It's the ability to accept that you don't need to be in the market constantly to make money. It's understanding that the best opportunities often take time to develop. And it's trusting your plan enough to not feel the need to rush it. If you can cultivate this mindset, you'll not only protect your capital, but you'll also improve your ability to make rational, consistent decisions in an environment as chaotic as the market.

Avoid Emotional Trading

Emotional trading is one of the biggest enemies of any trader. No matter how good your strategy is, how many books you have read or how long you have been trading, if you let emotions take over, the result will be disastrous. The market has no emotions, it doesn't care what you feel or how you react. It is completely neutral. But we, as human beings, are loaded with emotions, and that can become a serious problem if we don't learn to control them.

Trading on emotion means making decisions based on fear, greed, hope, or even anger, rather than based on your plan and objective analysis. For example, when you lose a trade and feel the urge to immediately recoup your losses, you will likely enter a new trade without properly analyzing the market. This type of behavior, known as "revenge trading," is a sure recipe for increasing your losses.

On the other hand, greed can also cloud your judgment. Let's say you're in a winning trade. Your plan says you should get out at a certain point, but you decide to stay longer because you want to squeeze out every penny possible. The problem is that the market can change at any moment, and what was a solid profit can quickly turn into a loss. Greed makes you break your own rules and take unnecessary risks.

Fear is another emotion that can paralyze you. Maybe your analysis tells you that you should enter a trade, but the fear of losing money stops you. Or maybe you're already in a trade, and even though everything indicates that the market will move in your favor, you decide to close it early for fear of losing your accumulated profits. The result is that instead of following your plan, you allow your emotions to guide you, and this rarely ends well.

So how do you avoid emotional trading? The first step is to recognize that you can't completely eliminate emotions. We're human, and emotions are part of our nature. But what you can do is learn to manage them so they don't interfere with your decisions. This starts with having a clear plan and following it to the letter. A plan gives you an objective frame of reference to act upon, even when your emotions are at their highest.

For example, if your plan says you should exit a trade when the price hits a certain level, do so without hesitation. Don't let the hope that the market will go higher or the fear that it will go lower change your mind. The key is to trust your analysis and the rules you set when you were in a calm state of mind.

Another powerful tool to avoid emotional trading is to set clear limits before trading. This includes defining how much you are willing to lose on each trade, how long you plan to hold a position open, and what your profit targets are. These limits help you maintain discipline and prevent you from making impulsive decisions in the moment.

It's also essential to keep a trading journal. Writing down each trade, along with the reasons why you took it and how you felt at the time, will help you identify patterns in your behavior. You may find that you tend to trade impulsively after a loss or that you hold on to winning trades too long. By being aware of these patterns, you can take steps to correct them.

Stress management is another crucial aspect. Trading is an intense activity, and it's easy to feel overwhelmed when the market doesn't behave the way you expected. Practicing relaxation techniques, such as deep breathing or meditation, can help you stay calm even during difficult times. It's also important to take regular breaks and make sure you're not trading when you're tired or emotionally drained.

Remember that emotional trading not only affects your financial results, but also your mental well-being. Trading under constant stress or frustration can lead to burnout and make you lose your passion for trading. That's why it's crucial to take care of yourself and make sure you're in the right frame of mind before trading.

A common misconception is that only beginners are vulnerable to emotional trading. The reality is that even experienced traders can fall into this trap if they are not careful. You may have years of experience and a solid account, but if you allow greed or fear to take over, your results can quickly deteriorate.

Finally, it's important to accept that you can't control the market. No matter how good your analysis is or how much experience you have, there will always be factors that are beyond your control. Accepting this will help you release the emotional burden of trying to predict every market move. Instead of focusing on what you can't control, focus on what you can control: your strategy, your risk management, and your discipline.

Emotional trading is a problem that affects everyone at some point, but it doesn't have to be your downfall. With a solid plan, clear boundaries, good stress management, and a willingness to learn from your mistakes, you can minimize their impact and make more rational decisions. At the end of the day, the market doesn't reward those who react impulsively; it rewards those who trade with patience, logic, and self-control. And those are qualities that, while not born naturally, can be cultivated over time.

Market News and Events Management

In trading, news and market events are like waves in the ocean: sometimes small and manageable, other times huge and dangerous. They can move prices in seconds, defying even the most detailed analysis. If you don't know how to handle them, news can become a death trap for your account. But if you learn to manage them correctly, you can avoid unpleasant surprises and sometimes even use them to your advantage.

To start, it's important to understand that not all news has the same impact. Some can move the market significantly, such as US employment reports, central bank interest rate decisions or unexpected announcements from major companies. Others, such as minor political statements or unconfirmed rumors, tend to have a more limited impact. The key is to identify which news is really important and which you can ignore.

The first step to managing the news is to be informed. This doesn't mean you should spend all day reading every headline that appears in the media, but you do need to have an up-to-date economic calendar and know what events are scheduled for each day. Economic calendars often highlight the most important events and rank their potential impact on the market. For example, an inflation report may have a high impact, while a political meeting may have a low impact. Having this information allows you to prepare and plan your trades.

When you know that a major news story is coming, it's crucial to adjust your strategy. One of the first decisions you need to make is whether you want to trade during the event or stay on the sidelines. Many experienced traders prefer not to trade during high-impact news, because market movements can be extremely volatile and difficult to predict. At such times, prices can move violently in both directions, triggering stop losses before you have a chance to react. If you decide not to trade, make sure to close your positions before the event to avoid unnecessary risk.

On the other hand, if you decide to trade during the news, you need to be aware of the risks and have a solid plan. In these cases, it is essential to reduce the size of your positions to limit potential losses. Also, consider widening your stop loss levels to give the market more room and avoid being wiped out by sudden moves. However, this should be done carefully, as widening your stop loss also means you are taking on a higher risk per trade.

Another key strategy is to avoid trading in the moments immediately before and after a major news event. Just before the announcement, the market often enters a state of anticipation, with erratic movements that do not follow any clear logic. After the announcement, the market may react unexpectedly, even if the results were predictable. This happens because it is not only the content of the news that matters, but also how it compares to market expectations. For example, if a central bank keeps interest rates as expected, the market could react negatively if traders were expecting signs of a future change.

In addition to scheduled news, such as economic reports and central bank decisions, you should also be prepared for unexpected news. These can include natural disasters, geopolitical conflicts, or surprise announcements from major companies. While it is impossible to predict these events, you can limit their impact on your account by following strict risk management rules, such as never risking more than a small percentage of your capital on a single trade.

A common mistake among beginner traders is to try to interpret all the news and use it as a basis for their trades. The problem is that not all news has a clear or immediate impact on the market. Also, markets don't always react the way you might expect. For example, positive news about a country's economy doesn't always lead to an increase in the value of its currency, because other factors are also at play.

That's why, instead of trying to predict how the market will react to a piece of news, it's better to focus on how the market is reacting in real time. Watch price action and look for clear signals before making decisions. This is called trading the reaction rather than the news. Instead of guessing, you're letting the market show you where it wants to go.

Another important aspect of managing the news is staying calm. High-impact events can be exciting, but they are also times when it's easy to lose your cool. Watching a fast-moving chart can make you want to jump in right away so you don't "miss out on the action." However, these impulsive decisions often lead to costly mistakes. Take a moment to breathe, analyze the situation, and stick to your plan.

Finally, remember that news and market events are only part of the bigger picture. While they can cause significant short-term moves, most long-term trends are driven by broader fundamental and technical factors. Don't obsess over every news story and instead focus on trading according to your strategy and long-term goals.

Managing market news and events isn't about avoiding risk altogether, but rather managing it intelligently. If you can learn to identify important events, adjust your strategy, and maintain discipline, you'll be better prepared to face the challenges and opportunities that arise in such a dynamic market. In the end, the goal isn't to beat the market, but to trade with confidence and consistency, even in the most uncertain times.

How to Design a Foolproof Trading Plan

Having a solid trading plan is like building a house on a firm foundation. Without a plan, your decisions will be based on impulses, emotions, and assumptions, which will sooner or later lead to costly mistakes. Designing a foolproof trading plan doesn't mean you'll never experience losses, but it will allow you to minimize risks and act consistently, even in the most unpredictable market conditions. This chapter will help you understand how to create a detailed, practical, and adaptable plan that will serve as a compass on your path as a trader.

The first step in designing a trading plan is to define your goals. This goes beyond just saying "I want to make money." Your goals should be specific, measurable, and realistic. For example, you could set goals like making a certain percentage of your bankroll per month or reducing your losses to less than a certain percentage per trade. It's also important to think about your long-term goals: are you looking to become a professional trader or just supplement your current income? Being clear about your goals will help you structure your plan around them.

Once you have your goals clear, the next step is to define your strategy. This is where you decide how and when to trade. Your strategy should be based on a detailed analysis of the markets you plan to trade. This includes identifying which financial instruments you are going to trade, what time frames you prefer, and what type of analysis you will use, whether technical, fundamental, or a combination of both. For example, you might decide to trade stocks based on technical analysis, using four-hour charts and looking for breakout patterns.

It's important to keep your strategy simple and to be able to explain it in just a few sentences. If you need too many conditions to justify a trade, it will be difficult to follow your plan consistently. Also, you should test your strategy before implementing it with real money. This is called backtesting, and it involves applying your strategy to historical data to see how it would have performed in the past. While backtesting doesn't guarantee future results, it will give you insight into the viability of your strategy and help you identify potential weaknesses.

The third component of a foolproof trading plan is risk management. This is probably the most important aspect of your plan, because even the best strategy can fail if you don't know how to manage risk. A fundamental rule is to never risk more than a small percentage of your capital on a single trade, usually between one and three percent. This ensures that you can survive a losing streak without destroying your account.

Additionally, you need to set clear rules for determining your position sizes. This is known as position size management and is directly related to the level of risk you are willing to take. For example, if you have a ten thousand dollar account and you decide to risk two percent per trade, this means that you should not lose more than two hundred dollars on any one trade. From this number, you can calculate your position size depending on the stop loss level you choose.

A good trading plan should also include rules for market entries and exits. This means defining the exact conditions that must be met before you open a position and the criteria you will use to close it. For example, you might decide to enter a trade only when a price breaks a key support level on high volume, and exit if the price retraces beyond a specific level. Having these rules will help you avoid impulsiveness and maintain discipline, even in times of high volatility.

Another key element of your plan is emotional management. The market will test your emotions over and over again, and if you're not prepared, it's easy to fall into destructive behavior patterns. Your plan should include strategies for staying calm, such as taking a break after a series of losses or setting time limits for your trading sessions. You can also include reminders for yourself, such as writing down your most important rules and keeping them in sight as you trade.

Additionally, a foolproof trading plan must be flexible. Markets are constantly changing, and a strategy that works well today might not be effective tomorrow. This doesn't mean you should change your plan every time you have a loss, but you should be willing to review and adjust it periodically. For example, you could evaluate your plan every three months to make sure it's still relevant and adapt it as needed.

Keeping a detailed record of your trades is also essential. A trading journal will allow you to analyze what you are doing well and what you need to improve. In your journal, write down every trade, including the reason you entered, how you felt during the trade, and how it ended. Over time, this record will become a valuable tool for learning from your mistakes and reinforcing your strengths.

Finally, remember that success in trading is not measured only by the profits you generate, but by your ability to trade consistently and disciplined over time. A foolproof trading plan is not a guarantee of immediate success, but it is a solid foundation on which you can build a profitable career. The key is to follow your plan rigorously, learn from every experience, and never stop improving.

Designing a trading plan may seem like a tedious job, but it is an investment in your future as a trader. It is the map that will guide you through a path full of uncertainty and help you avoid impulsive and costly decisions. In the end, the time and effort you put into building a solid plan will save you years of frustration and avoidable mistakes. So take the time, be honest with yourself, and create a plan that will become your best ally in the market.

The Advantage of Backtesting and Forward Testing

When it comes to trading, there is no room for guesswork or impromptu experiments with real money. A strategy that has not been properly tested is like driving a car with your eyes closed, hoping for everything to work out. This is where two essential tools for any trader come into play: backtesting and forward testing. These processes not only help you validate your strategy, but they also build your confidence and prepare you to face the markets with a more professional and disciplined approach.

Backtesting, as the name suggests, is about testing a strategy using historical market data. Basically, you take your strategy and see how it would have performed in the past. This allows you to analyse its performance under different market conditions without risking any real money. But it's not just about looking at numbers and charts; it's about understanding whether your strategy is robust, consistent and capable of generating positive results over time. The goal isn't to find a strategy that never loses, because that doesn't exist, but to make sure that the gains consistently outweigh the losses.

To perform effective backtesting, you need to be very clear about the rules of your strategy. For example, if your strategy says to enter a trade when the price crosses the 50-period moving average upwards, then you must apply that exact rule to historical data. Don't adjust the rules as you go or make exceptions. The purpose of backtesting is to evaluate the strategy as it is defined, not to force it to fit the results you want to see.

Backtesting not only shows you whether your strategy is profitable, but it also helps you understand its weak points. You might find that it works well in trending markets, but not in sideways markets. Or you might find that transaction costs, such as spreads and commissions, significantly reduce your profits. These discoveries are valuable because they allow you to fine-tune your strategy and improve it before implementing it in real time.

Once you have backtested and have positive results, the next step is forward testing. This process involves testing your strategy in real-time, but in a controlled environment, such as a demo account. This is where you bring your strategy into the present and see how it performs in current market conditions. Unlike backtesting, where you know the outcome because the data is historical, in forward testing you are facing the uncertainty of the market in real-time. This allows you to assess not only the effectiveness of your strategy, but also your ability to execute it correctly.

Forward testing is especially useful for identifying issues that might not be apparent in backtesting. For example, you might find that it's difficult to follow your rules when the market is moving quickly, or that you need to adjust your stop loss levels because the current market has more volatility than the historical data you used. It also helps you assess how you handle emotions when trading, since even though you're not risking real money, the pressure of making decisions in real time is still there.

One of the key benefits of forward testing is that it forces you to be disciplined. When you trade on a demo account, you must treat it as if it were real money. This means following your strategy to the letter, recording every trade, and avoiding making impulsive decisions. If you can't be disciplined on a demo account, it will be even harder to be disciplined with real money. Forward testing is, in many ways, training for the trader, helping you develop the right habits and identify any weaknesses in your approach.

Both processes, backtesting and forward testing, have a common goal: helping you trade with confidence. When you know your strategy has been tested and makes sense in different market conditions, it's much easier to stick with it, even when you're facing a losing streak. Without this testing, every loss feels like a personal blow and leaves you wondering if your strategy really works. But with data backing up your decisions, you can stay calm and trust that the process will pay off in the long run.

It is important to mention that both backtesting and forward testing have limitations. In the case of backtesting, you are working with historical data, which means that you cannot predict how the market will behave in the future. Markets are constantly changing, and a strategy that worked well in the past might not be effective in the present. On the other hand, forward testing requires time and patience, as you are testing your strategy in real time, and this can take weeks or months before you have enough data to evaluate its performance.

Also, you need to be wary of the trap of over-optimizing your strategy during backtesting. This is when you continually adjust the rules to perfectly fit historical data, creating a strategy that seems foolproof in the past, but is unlikely to work in the future. This problem, known as over-optimization or curve fitting, is one of the reasons why forward testing is so important. It is the final test to ensure that your strategy is viable under real-world conditions.

In short, backtesting and forward testing are essential tools for any serious trader. Not only do they help you validate your ideas and improve your strategies, but they also mentally prepare you to trade with confidence and discipline. These processes require time, effort, and attention to detail, but the benefits are invaluable. Trading without testing is like playing the lottery; trading with a proven plan is like running a well-planned business. If you are willing to invest the time necessary to test your strategies, you will be one step closer to becoming a consistent and profitable trader.

How to Handle Losing Streaks

Losing streaks are an unavoidable reality in trading. Even the most experienced traders, with proven strategies and years of practice, face times when it seems like nothing is working. It's important to understand that a losing streak doesn't define your skill as a trader, but it can test your mindset, your discipline, and your ability to keep going. In this chapter, we're going to explore how to effectively handle these streaks so they don't destroy your confidence or your account.

The first thing you need to do is accept that losses are a natural part of trading. No matter how good your strategy is or how disciplined you are, there will always be factors outside of your control that can lead to negative results. This doesn't mean you're doing anything wrong. It's simply the nature of the market, which is unpredictable and often volatile. Accepting this from the start will help you not to take losses personally. The market isn't against you, it's just doing what it always does: moving in all directions.

When you're in the midst of a losing streak, it's crucial to stay calm and not panic. Panic leads to impulsive decisions, such as increasing your position size to try to recoup your losses or changing your strategy in the heat of the moment. These emotional reactions almost always end up making the situation worse. Instead of reacting, stop and evaluate. Ask yourself if you're following your trading plan or if you've strayed. Sometimes, a losing streak is simply the result of unfavorable market conditions, and not a mistake on your part.

One of the most important steps to take in handling a losing streak is to reduce your risk exposure. If you're used to risking two percent of your capital per trade, consider reducing it to one percent or even less while things stabilize. This will allow you to continue trading without the constant fear that a single trade could cause significant damage to your account. Reducing risk also gives you the mental space to analyze the situation objectively, without the pressure of large potential losses.

Another effective strategy is to take a break. When losses are piling up, it's easy to fall into a negative emotional state where every decision is influenced by fear or frustration. At these times, stepping away from the market can be the best thing you can do. A break gives you a chance to clear your mind, review your trading plan, and analyze your recent trades without the urgency of making real-time decisions. Returning to the market with a fresh mindset can make a huge difference in your performance.

During a losing streak, it's essential to review your trades to identify patterns or recurring mistakes. This doesn't mean you should question every detail of your strategy, but you should look for signs that something might be going wrong. Maybe you're entering trades too early or late, or maybe the market has changed in a way that makes your current strategy not as effective. Use a trading journal to record every trade, including the reasons behind your decisions and how you felt at the time. This analysis can reveal adjustments you need to make to improve.

It's also important to remember that losing streaks don't just affect your account, they also affect your confidence. When things aren't going well, it's easy to start doubting your abilities and wondering if you really have what it takes to be successful at trading. During these times, it's crucial to focus on the aspects of the process that you can control, such as following your trading plan and maintaining discipline. Focus on the right actions, not the short-term results. Trading is a long-term game, and a losing streak is just a small part of that journey.

Setting limits for your daily, weekly, or monthly losses can be another useful tool for managing losing streaks. For example, you might decide that if you lose a certain percentage of your account in a day, you will stop trading until the next day. This prevents emotions from taking over and you from trying to recoup losses in a suboptimal state of mind. Similarly, if you hit a weekly or monthly loss limit, you might take a longer break to reevaluate your approach.

The right mindset also plays a crucial role in how you handle losing streaks. Instead of seeing them as a failure, try to view them as an opportunity to learn and improve. Every loss contains a lesson, whether it's about the market, your strategy, or your own emotions. If you can extract those lessons and apply them in the future, even the most painful losses will serve a valuable purpose in your development as a trader.

Finally, surround yourself with support. Trading can be a lonely business, and during a losing streak, that loneliness can amplify your negative emotions. Talking to other traders, a mentor, or even friends and family who understand your goals can help put things into perspective. Knowing that you're not alone and that others have been through the same thing can be a source of motivation and reassurance.

In short, managing losing streaks requires a combination of acceptance, analysis, and discipline. You can't avoid them entirely, but you can reduce their impact on your account and your mindset. By staying calm, reducing risk, taking breaks, and learning from each experience, you can turn a difficult situation into an opportunity to grow and become stronger as a trader. Remember that success in trading is not measured by the absence of losses, but by how you respond to them and how you keep moving forward despite the challenges.

Accepting that Losses are Part of the Game

Accepting that losses are part of the game is one of the most important steps to becoming a successful trader. It may sound counterintuitive. After all, the goal of trading is to make money, not lose it. However, this mindset is precisely what separates traders who fail from those who thrive. Those who obsess over avoiding losses at all costs often make mistakes like moving their stop losses, holding onto losing positions for too long, or risking more than they should. These behaviors, ironically, end up leading to more losses.

The first thing you need to understand is that losses are not a reflection of your skill or worth as a person. They are a natural consequence of trading in an uncertain environment. The market is full of variables that you cannot control, such as unexpected news, sudden changes in volatility, and moves that defy any technical or fundamental analysis. Even with a solid strategy, there will be times when everything seems to align, and yet the market moves against you. This does not mean that you have done anything wrong. It simply means that trading, like any other probability-based activity, includes the risk of losing.

Accepting losses as a normal part of the process is essential because it frees you from the pressure of trying to be perfect. Perfection is an unrealistic expectation that only leads to frustration. No one, not even the most successful traders in the world, has a loss-free trading record. What sets great traders apart is not their ability to avoid losses, but their ability to manage them in an intelligent and emotionally balanced manner. They understand that they don't need to win every trade to be profitable. What matters is that, on average, their wins are greater than their losses.

An effective way to accept losses is to change the way you interpret them. Instead of seeing them as failures, see them as the cost of doing business in the financial markets. Just as an entrepreneur has to invest in inventory, advertising, or personnel, a trader has to invest in the process of trading, and that includes accepting losses. Every trade you make has a cost associated with it, and sometimes that cost is a loss. If you think about it this way, a loss is just a natural part of the process.

It is important to mention that accepting losses does not mean resigning yourself to losing money uncontrollably. Quite the opposite. Acceptance allows you to face losses with a clearer and more rational mindset. When you understand that losses are inevitable, you become more proactive in risk management. You set stop loss levels, define how much you are willing to risk per trade, and follow your trading plan without deviation. This preparation protects you from catastrophic losses and gives you the confidence that even if you lose on a trade, you will not be putting your capital at risk.

Another key to accepting losses is understanding that not every trade has to be a winner for you to be a profitable trader. For example, if you have a strategy that wins on 50 percent of trades but your profits are twice your average losses, you will be profitable over the long term. This concept, known as mathematical expectation, is fundamental to trading. By focusing on the bigger picture rather than obsessing over each individual trade, you can trade with more calm and less stress.

It's also helpful to remember that losses can teach you valuable lessons. Every time you lose, you have an opportunity to learn something new about the market, your strategy, or even yourself. You might find that you're not managing your emotions well or that you're entering trades on impulse. Or you might realize that your strategy needs tweaking to better suit certain market conditions. If you adopt the mindset that every loss is a learning opportunity, you'll begin to view them as a valuable part of your development as a trader.

One of the biggest obstacles to accepting losses is ego. We all want to be right, and in trading this manifests itself in the desire for every trade to be successful. However, the market does not reward ego. In fact, trading with the goal of proving you are right often leads to holding losing positions for too long or opening impulsive trades to try to recoup losses. Ego has no place in trading. Instead of focusing on being right, focus on trading in a disciplined and consistent manner.

Accepting losses also has a positive effect on your mental health. Trading under the constant fear of losing is exhausting and can lead to emotional burnout. When you accept losses as a natural part of trading, you reduce the pressure you put on yourself and allow yourself to trade with a more relaxed mindset. This not only improves your performance, but also makes the process of trading more sustainable and enjoyable in the long run.

In short, accepting that losses are part of the game is a mindset shift that can completely transform your approach to trading. It's not about minimizing their impact, but rather understanding that they are inevitable and manageable. By stopping fighting the reality of losses, you can focus on what really matters: managing risk, sticking to your plan, and learning from every experience. Ultimately, success in trading is not measured by the absence of losses, but by your ability to effectively manage them and keep moving toward your goals.

Avoid Overconfidence After Earnings

One of the biggest dangers for any trader is not facing a losing streak, but what happens after a winning streak. Overconfidence is a silent trap that can destroy everything you have achieved if you do not learn to control it. It is natural to feel invincible after a series of successful trades, but this feeling can lead you to make mistakes that risk your capital and your emotional stability. Recognizing and managing overconfidence is essential to maintaining consistency in trading.

The problem with overconfidence is that it distorts your perception of reality. After several winning trades, it's easy to start believing that you have everything under control, that you've mastered the market, or that your skills are above average. This overconfidence can cause you to make impulsive decisions, such as increasing your position sizes, trading with less analysis, or ignoring your risk rules. The worst thing is that, in the moment, these actions may seem completely reasonable because your confidence makes you feel like nothing can go wrong.

Overconfidence can also lead you to think that the market owes you something, as if profits are the result of your genius rather than a combination of skill, strategy, and in many cases, a little luck. The market does not operate under the rules of your ego. It is unpredictable, and the next trade has no relation to the previous ones. Believing that you are on an unstoppable streak is a recipe for disaster because it makes you forget the fundamental: every trade has risk, and every decision must be made with care and discipline.

One of the biggest risks of overconfidence is that it causes you to let your guard down. Maybe you decide to skip an important part of your analysis because you think you already understand enough. Maybe you enter a trade without a clear plan because you assume your intuition will suffice. Or worse, maybe you start trading outside of your strategy because you feel like whatever you do will be a success. These behaviors may seem small at first, but each one represents a breakdown in the discipline you need to survive as a long-term trader.

The key to avoiding overconfidence is to always remember that trading isn't about winning a series of trades, but rather maintaining consistency over time. Even the best strategies will have periods where they don't work out the way you expected, and market conditions are constantly changing. Recognizing this helps you stay humble and respect the process rather than obsessing over short-term results.

Another effective way to manage overconfidence is to set clear rules for your trading, even after a series of wins. These rules may include limits on your position sizes, restrictions on the number of trades you can make in a day, or a mandatory pause after reaching a certain level of profit. These measures are not meant to punish you, but to protect you from yourself when euphoria starts to cloud your judgment.

Keeping a trading journal can also be a valuable tool for managing overconfidence. After each trade, record not only the results, but also your thoughts, emotions, and reasons for taking that trade. Reviewing this journal will help you identify patterns in your behavior. You may notice that after a particularly large trade, you tend to make riskier decisions. Being aware of these tendencies gives you the opportunity to correct them before they cause problems.

It's important to mention that feeling good after a win isn't a bad thing in itself. In fact, you should celebrate your achievements, but in moderation. Recognize that one winning trade doesn't guarantee that the next one will be a winner. Humility is your best ally in trading, because it keeps you alert and prepared for anything the market throws at you. Arrogance, on the other hand, makes you vulnerable.

Another practical tip is to surround yourself with reminders of your past losses. This doesn't mean you should live in fear, but you should use your negative experiences as a counterweight to balance your confidence. Reviewing trades where you made mistakes can help you stay grounded and remember that no one is invincible in the market. Not only does this keep you focused, but it also reinforces the importance of following your rules and respecting risk.

Finally, it is crucial to separate your emotions from the trading process. It is easy to let pride and excitement take over after a winning streak, but trading should not be driven by emotions, whether positive or negative. A balanced mindset is what will allow you to make objective and rational decisions, even in times when everything seems to be going in your favor.

Overconfidence is a constant threat in trading, but you can combat it with a combination of humility, discipline, and self-awareness. Acknowledge your accomplishments, but don't let them define your perception of yourself as a trader. Every trade is a new opportunity to keep learning, growing, and improving. Keep the focus on the process, not the immediate results, and remember that trading success is not a sprint, but a marathon. True achievement is in consistency, not the fleeting thrill of a winning streak.

How to Evaluate Your Performance as a Defensive Trader

Evaluating your performance as a defensive trader is a crucial task that goes far beyond looking at your account balance. While it is tempting to measure your success solely by profits, this approach does not fully reflect your progress or guarantee that you are trading sustainably. As a defensive trader, your primary goal is not just to win, but to preserve your capital while looking for growth opportunities. To do this, you need a detailed and structured approach that allows you to analyze every aspect of your performance.

The first step in evaluating your performance is to track all relevant data from your trades. This includes entries, exits, position sizes, stop loss levels, profit targets, and any adjustments you made during the trade. But don't stop there. It's also critical to record the context of the trade, such as market conditions, the reasons behind your decision, and your emotional state at the time. This level of detail may seem overwhelming at first, but it's a goldmine of information that will help you identify patterns and areas for improvement.

An essential metric for a defensive trader is drawdown. This term refers to the amount of capital you lose from a high point to a low point in a specific period. Evaluating your drawdown is key because it shows you how you handle losses and whether you are risking more than you should. Excessive drawdown can indicate that you are trading too aggressively or that you are not managing your risk well. On the other hand, keeping a low drawdown shows that you are protecting your capital effectively, even during difficult periods.

Another important metric is your average risk-reward ratio. As a defensive trader, you should make sure that the potential profits from your trades are significantly greater than the potential losses. This doesn't mean that you need to win on every trade, but it does mean that, on average, your profits more than offset your losses. If you find that this ratio is not favorable, it may be time to review your strategy or adjust your entry and exit levels.

The win rate, or percentage of winning trades, is another statistic that deserves attention, but it shouldn't be your only focus. Many traders fall into the trap of obsessing over having a high win rate, but this doesn't always translate into profitability. For example, you could win on 80 percent of your trades and still lose money if your losses are much larger than your wins. It's not how many trades you win that matters, but how you manage the balance between wins and losses.

Consistency is another key factor when evaluating your performance. Are you following your trading plan in a disciplined manner or do you frequently deviate? Are you taking consistent risks or do you sometimes trade impulsively? Reviewing your trades for signs of consistency will help you measure your progress as a defensive trader. If you find that you are acting inconsistently, this may be a sign that you need to work on your discipline or adjust your mindset.

It's also critical to assess your emotional management. How do you react after a losing trade? Do you get carried away by euphoria after a win? Your ability to stay calm and trade rationally is just as important as any financial metric. If you notice that your emotions are influencing your decisions, this is something you should address immediately, perhaps with techniques such as meditation, journaling, or simply taking a break from the market.

Analyzing your mistakes is also part of evaluation. It's not about beating yourself up, but about learning. Every mistake is an opportunity to improve. Review your losing trades and ask yourself if you followed your plan, ignored any important signals, or let your emotions dictate your actions. Sometimes a loss can simply be the result of market randomness, but other times it can reveal a weakness in your strategy or approach.

Of course, you should also analyze your winning trades. It's easy to assume that everything you did on a winning trade was correct, but this isn't always the case. Maybe you took an unnecessary risk that turned out well by chance. Evaluating your winning trades in the same level of detail as your losing ones will allow you to identify whether you're sticking to your plan or just getting lucky.

An invaluable tool for evaluating your performance is a trading journal. This journal should not only include the technical data of your trades, but also your thoughts, emotions, and observations. Over time, this record will allow you to identify patterns in your behavior and the performance of your strategy. For example, you might find that you tend to trade better at certain times or under certain market conditions. Or you might notice that you always make the same mistakes after a winning streak. This level of self-awareness is essential to your growth as a trader.

Finally, remember that evaluating your performance as a defensive trader isn't something you do once. It's an ongoing process that takes time and dedication. Set a regular schedule to review your trades, perhaps at the end of each week or month, and use this review to adjust your approach as needed. The goal isn't to be perfect, but to continually improve.

In trading, as in life, progress is not linear. There will be ups and downs, and that's okay. The important thing is to stay focused on the process and not get discouraged by setbacks or blinded by successes. Evaluating yourself regularly will help you stay on track and develop the skills and mindset needed to succeed in the long run. At the end of the day, being a defensive trader isn't about avoiding risk altogether, but about managing it intelligently and consistently. And the only way to do that is by keeping a clear and honest view of your performance.

Evolving from a Defensive Trader to a Consistent Trader

Being a defensive trader is a great achievement. You've learned how to protect your capital, control risk, and stay calm in an environment that can be chaotic. But at some point, you may feel like you're stuck, like you're stuck in a cycle where you're simply surviving rather than thriving. This is the time to take the next step: evolving from a defensive trader to a consistent trader. This shift isn't about taking on more risk or chasing quick wins, but about developing a more balanced and sustainable approach that combines defense with calculated offense.

Consistency in trading doesn't mean you'll always win. It means you'll always trade according to a plan, you'll make decisions based on logic and strategy, not emotion, and your results will be predictable in the sense that they reflect a disciplined application of your method. The first step in evolving toward this consistency is to strengthen your mindset. As a defensive trader, you already understand the importance of protecting your capital, but now you must focus on building confidence in your system. This takes time, patience, and practice.

A consistent trader understands that his success does not depend on a single trade, but on the aggregate of all his trades over time. To achieve this, you need a solid trading plan, but you must also commit to following it without deviation. This is where many traders fail. After a few losses, they begin to doubt their strategy and make impulsive adjustments, losing their way. Consistency requires that you trust your plan even when things don't go your way. This doesn't mean you should never make changes, but any adjustments should be based on objective analysis, not an emotional reaction.

Another key aspect of becoming a consistent trader is understanding the importance of expectation management. In trading, the reality is that you are not going to win every day, every week, or even every month. There will be ups and downs, and accepting this will help you stay calm and avoid impulsive decisions. A consistent trader does not obsess over short-term results. Instead, they evaluate their performance over longer periods and focus on improving little by little.

Consistency is also based on discipline, and discipline is strengthened through repetition. Every time you stick to your trading plan, even when the market goes against you, you are strengthening your self-discipline. Every time you stop to analyze a trade before entering, rather than jumping in impulsively, you are building the foundation for a consistent approach. It's not about perfection, because no one is perfect at trading, but it is about commitment to a well-thought-out process.

To evolve toward consistency, you also need to be honest with yourself. Keeping a trading journal is one of the most valuable tools you can use. Write down not only your trades, but also your thoughts, emotions, and observations. Over time, this record will become a mirror that shows you where you are being consistent and where you are not. You may find that you keep deviating from your plan after a losing streak or that you trade more aggressively when you are excited. Being aware of these patterns is the first step to correcting them.

Patience is another pillar of consistency. As a defensive trader, you've probably already learned to wait for the best setups rather than jumping at every opportunity that appears. However, evolving toward consistency means taking this patience to the next level. Sometimes, this involves not trading at all for days or even weeks if the market doesn't present clear opportunities. It can be hard to resist the temptation to act, especially when you see other traders posting impressive gains, but patience is what will allow you to avoid costly mistakes and stay in the game for the long haul.

One aspect that distinguishes consistent traders is their ability to handle both winning and losing streaks with the same balanced mindset. After a winning streak, they don't let euphoria lead them to take unnecessary risks. After a losing streak, they don't sink into despair or try to recoup losses quickly. Instead, they remain focused on their plan and methodically executing their strategy. This emotional balance is what allows them to remain consistent in all market conditions.

Consistency is also built through adaptation. The market is constantly changing, and what works today may not work tomorrow. As a defensive trader, you already have the advantage of being cautious, but now you need to complement this caution with the ability to adapt when necessary. This doesn't mean abandoning your strategy as soon as you face difficulties, but rather being willing to objectively analyze what is working and what isn't, and adjust your approach as needed.

Finally, evolving towards consistency means accepting that this process has no end. There will always be something to learn, something to improve, and something to adjust. Even the most successful traders in the world never stop working on their development. Consistency is not a destination, but rather a continuous journey. It is a daily commitment to your growth as a trader and as a person.

Ultimately, being a consistent trader means trading with confidence, but also with humility. It's knowing that each trade is just a small part of a bigger picture. It's accepting that you can't control the market, but you can control how you react to it. And it's always remembering that your success isn't just measured in dollars and cents, but in your ability to trade in a disciplined, methodical, and sustainable manner. With every step you take toward consistency, you'll be building not only your success as a trader, but also a solid foundation for achieving your long-term goals.

www.ingramcontent.com/pod-product-compliance
Lightning Source LLC
LaVergne TN
LVHW090424210926
848480LV00002B/669